AF097257

<u>Dedicated To:</u>
My sister, Mary

<u>Written By:</u> Abigail Gartland

Hello, my name is St. Bernadette!

I was born in Lourdes, France on January 7, 1844.

One day, when I was a young girl, I went to collect some firewood for my family.

As I was standing there, a beautiful figure appeared to me.

This holy lady was Mary, the Mother of God. She asked me to come visit her every day and to pray for sinners.

I returned each day, and I brought friends with me to see her.

I was very confused, but I dug into the mud. When I returned the next day, all the mud had turned to water!

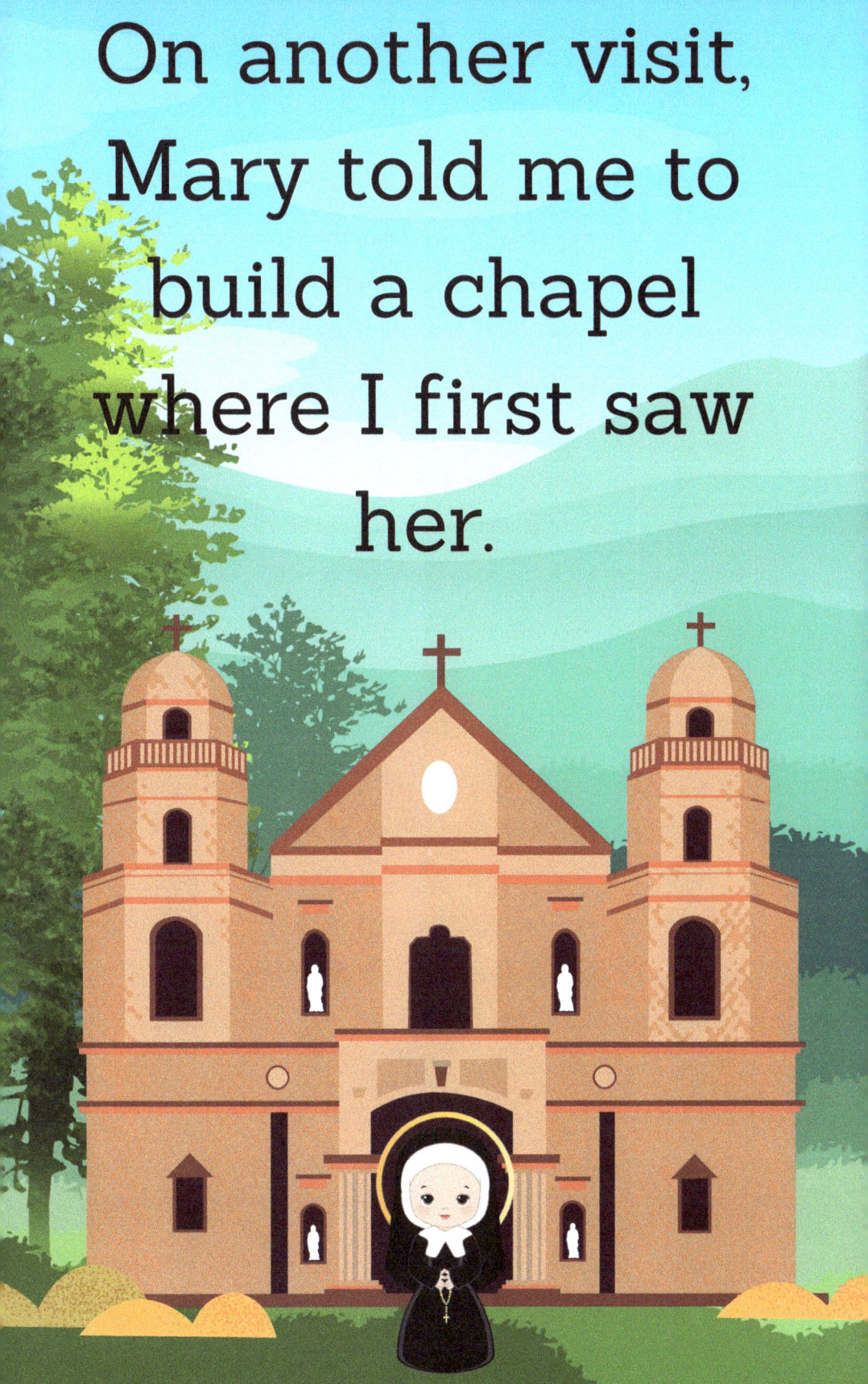

After I saw Mary many times, I decided to become a Sister of Charity.

I worked with the Sisters of Charity to help the poor and needy in the name of God.

I spent the rest of my days with the sisters in prayer to Jesus.

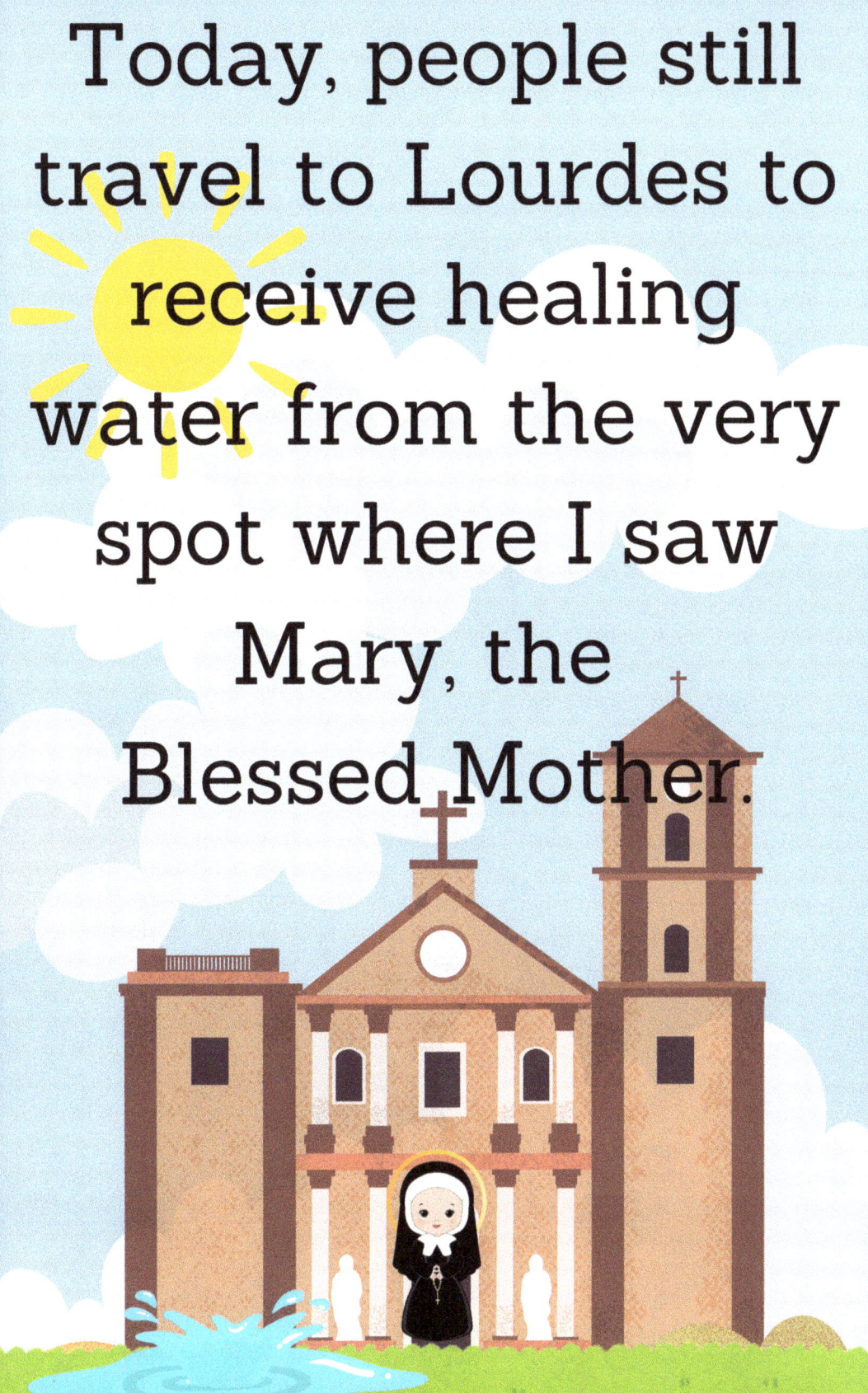

Today, people still travel to Lourdes to receive healing water from the very spot where I saw Mary, the Blessed Mother.

I went to Heaven on April 16, 1879 to spend eternity with Mary and Jesus.

Do you want to be more like me?

You can celebrate my feast day with me on April 16th.

I am the patron saint of the poor, sickness, and Lourdes, France.

I pray for you every day of your life.

St. Bernadette, pray for us!

Copyright:

Clipart: © PentoolPixie © LimeandKiwiDesigns
Licensed purchased: 1/10/2024

About the Author

Abigail Gartland

I love the saints and I love my faith. The idea for sharing the stories of the saints with little ones came when my dear friends were expecting their first baby. I wanted to create something as unique and special as our friendship. Each book is dedicated to very special people and groups who have enriched my faith in different ways. I am blessed to write these stories and appreciate the unending support of my family and friends. When I am not writing, I am a middle school teacher. I hope you enjoy these stories. I pray for each and every person who opens one of my books to learn more about the saints.

Abbie

www.ingramcontent.com/pod-product-compliance
Lightning Source LLC
LaVergne TN
LVHW061632070526
838199LV00071B/6657